The 8 Most Practical Tips On How to Meet, Attract and Seduce Any Woman: How to Be Naturally Masculine and Interesting in Front of the Woman of Your Dreams

MATEO LAMBERT

DEDICATION

This book is dedicated to all men who have decided to work on themselves and become better, as well as to all women who give us the strongest motivation for this.

CONTENTS

"Every man has the right to risk his own life in order to preserve it. Has it ever been said that a man who throws himself out the window to escape from a fire is guilty of suicide?"

—Jean-Jacques Rousseau

THE DECISION

Everything happened just when I realize and accept this - I don't know how to behave with the girls that I like. And awareness of this came later than I would want but it had its own reasons.

Since school years, like many teenagers, I was interested in girls. Although, in truth, they paid more attention to me than the other way around. And it's normal for guys at a certain age. I would not say that I avoided contact with my female peers, but considered them purely as friends, along with the male peers. But the years passed, and in a time when many of my friends began to move, so to speak, on a different level of communication with the girls, on the contrary, I began to move away from it. I was completely captured by the sport. Day and night, I dreamed of a hockey player's career and I was not interested in anything else. I thought that all these relations were unnecessary and took a lot of time. Now, I realize that I was wrong. After all, the relationship between a boy and a girl, a man and a woman - it is our nature, we have been created in such a way. Whether it is an innocent flirtation or sexual desire - this is very important. It is important not only in the present but in the future when you decide to create your family.

I achieved my goal, and due to a sports scholarship entered to university. I continued to play and get pleasure from it all. Then I met a girl, we spent 3 years together. In truth, the beginning of our relationship was her merit. I especially didn't make any effort to our relationships, it was good and most importantly, easy. Nearby was a beautiful girl who loved me, and I in turn, loved her.

Sports career for a number of reasons was coming to an end, along as the study at the university, and it was time to think about the future. Next door was the same girl I increasingly felt that we will be together until the end of life. And I was beginning to wonder if she is not against me to become my wife. She was an important person to me, and I believed that we would be together forever.

And in one moment everything collapsed. I received an email from anonymous, which was full of mildly erotic photos. On those photos was my girlfriend with some sort of old men, about 20 years older than her. Well, there were a couple of videos in addition. With them. It turned out this message has come not only to me but also to all our common friends. It was a complete shock. I still do not know who did it and why. I was crushed and depressed, but the most important thing I could not understand her reasons for such action. I thought everything between us was just great. But as it turned out, it was all a game. There were no any explanations from her. We strongly quarreled, she made me guilty. She only said that it was her past, she had to somehow earn money, but now she loves me and wants to be only with me. All anything, but the photo and video is clearly visible - they are made recently. We broke up, and it was a big morale blow for me. For a few months, I was in complete bewilderment, not knowing what to do next. After this incident, I realized that I do not understand women. And this will be difficult to live with...

Moving away from everything that happened, I decided that I didn't want to look for the girl who is the one and only, but now it would be better to try to interact with all of who I like. I was keenly aware that I did not understand the psychology of women, their motivations and the reasons for their various actions. I needed a lot more experience with women to understand what I want and who I want. I was a good student in college, I had a good sports reputation, in the end, I lived 3 years with a girl. I felt like I was a normal man and I deserve a lot of girls that I like. But my understanding of yourself is one thing, but in practice, it turned out that everything is much sadder. No need to say that I couldn't drag someone into bed, I couldn't conduct even a five-minute conversation. Again, I realized that I did not know anything about women: what they think, how they think, why they commit certain actions, and most importantly, what they are really looking for in men.

And in that moment, I made the decision for myself. I wanted to understand the nature of women, to understand what they want from men, and in the end, it was very important to me what type of a male they desire!

Going hard on the way of development in relationships with women, by lots of trials and errors, but at the same time, and thanks to the gradual progress, I realized how I was mistaken with regard to the psychology of women when I was younger, and at the time when I had a girl. How many things I did not know and understand would help me in all areas of life, not only in seducing beauties.

The process of my development after The Decision was very difficult. Every day, I literally put myself to the city to practice skills. From the very beginning, I practiced banal approaches, trying to start any conversation, and then gradually move on to practicing the skills of seduction of those girls that I liked. To do this I had to go out of my comfort zone every time I approached a new strange girl. My skills of dating women were so small that at first, I was uncomfortable to even think about such possibility of just walking up to a beautiful girl, and get acquainted. I was blushing, stammering and behaving like the last schoolboy. But after each situation, the boundaries of my comfort zone expanded. I did not pay attention to the refusal itself; I tried to understand the cause, and the cause of which was in me, in my behavior. After each analysis, my own mistakes and failures, I put more and more insane goals and tried by all means at any cost to achieve them. At first, I worked only on the quantity. I set a goal to get acquainted with 15-20 girls per day. There were days when I became acquainted with more than 50 girls...Step by step, I reached a level when I started to enjoy the pleasure of communicating with the girls. I began to read them, to anticipate the development of the dialogues in specific situations and to direct those same situations in my favor. I began to turn out to seduce most beautiful girls that I liked. Of course, the development process in this area is endless, and I still cannot say that I know all about seducing women. But the fact that from a complete zero, I became a man, that can talk with almost any girl, a man, who could, if he wanted to fuck a new girl every day, and a man who communicates with women easily and with pleasure, says that I have accumulated some experience, which I am delighted to share with. Therefore, to help you, my friends, I summarized my experience in 8 basic principles in dating and seducing women. 8 truths, in which I put all my experience. 8 things, using which you will definitely accelerate your way of becoming self-confident, attractive to women, male. Hurry up and read them to raise the level of your natural masculinity, and every beauty you were afraid to approach yesterday, will likely be in your bed!

1. DON'T HIDE YOUR INTENTIONS.

Most of my life, I felt some awkwardness and shyness when it comes to dating girls. I thought it was some awkward process that I impose to the person, and for my desire to even approach an unknown girl. I felt kind of ashamed! I was ashamed to show a girl that I like her, to show my sexual desire. In those rare moments when I still met with the girls, I said to myself, "I'll just talk to her," and we just talked, she told me about herself, I talked about myself, and that's it, nothing more! Besides, I was shy, unconfident, and often I only listened to the girl, only occasionally asking about something. Once I made the decision, and began to work on yourself, get out of your comfort zone (read about it a little further), and get the first results, I noticed that the girls do not like it when you're being uncertain, closed, and when they have no idea what your motives are. This causes negative suspicions.

I realized that to some extent, the girls like it when you show that you know what you want. Of course, we should not talk directly (at least at the very beginning of your relations) "I would fuck you nicely," but to deny it, at least for yourself - it is fundamentally wrong, my friend! After walking up to the girl with the intention of "just talking," you program your mind, and brain on this! And when talking with her, you will keep being an interlocutor, a nice and sweet guy, but that she does not need it! Believe me, she has it enough! Who she wants, so it's a male! And when you do not deny, at least, to ourselves that she is attractive, and you came to it, because you are sexually attracted to her, you will unconsciously behave like a real male! And believe me, she will feel it, and that's more than enough! Now I can speak on any topic, and behave as I want, but ultimately, I know that only one thing matters - whether she felt in you the male, masculinity, or not. So do not be afraid to show that she is attractive to you, because you are a man, you're a leader, and you set a vector of your further relationship!

4

Make things easier, friends, don't complicate them.

A couple of practical tips: keep a strong eye contact, do not be afraid of the opportunity to gently touch her, flirt with her, smile with her - it will definitely give her the feel that she is attractive to you, and that you want her as a woman! And the sooner she will feel it, the easier the things will be going! Of course, if she already has a long-term relationship, or something just like this, she, probably, will reject your intentions, (but not the fact) and nothing will happen. But if she is free, and sees you as an interesting, adequate man who knows what he wants, and at the same time gave her the feeling that he wants her, then, in such a situation, she is very likely to give you the opportunity to act!

2. DON'T BE ATTACHED TO THE RESULT! DON'T LET HER REJECTION TO HURT YOU.

Let's say you really like a girl, you want it, you imagine different scenarios, what will you do, and so on. You want your liking to be mutual, and this girl likes you, too. This is so, and that's fine. It is a natural human desire. But as soon as you fall in love with some kind of beauty, and you have a desire to be liked by her - you're a hostage of situation. You begin to adjust to the girl and start to agree with her in all (as I did), and thus you lose your rod, your reality and your Me. And in such a situation, with the happening of a negative reaction, I remember that I was upset, I began to blame myself. What does all - because of me. That failure - a sign that I was not good enough. And this emotional attachment to the result, to positive reaction, and thirst to be liked was a no for me, and I'm sure, it stops a lot of males. It makes you unnatural, by your trying to be cute for her - you get her to feel her dominance. But she wants to feel dominance from you, from the male! Women like when males make the decisions and are adamant to them.

Accordingly, what helped me a lot, and with what I want to share with you, is to accept this simple truth - that all around you - a lot of girls, just a huge number. And you have an infinite number of attempts. If It did not work with the one, you can always try another one. Because, look, you can get up now, go out, see a pretty girl - and get acquainted with her. If something goes wrong - you can walk 50 meters, and get acquainted with the another girl. And so on to infinity! To be attached to someone and be upset because of a failure with someone - is very stupid in a situation when you can always try again. A new attempt - the best attempt, because in it you will be with the experience of their past failures, respectively, you can make better decisions, and behave more appropriately. So do not get attached to the outcome, show girl - that you like her, but at the same time, emotionally, you are absolutely sure of himself, and her answer can't hurt you anyhow. She should not feel like a prize! At any time, you can get away from her, to the girl that is better. Do not forget this one!

3. BE NATURAL AND DON'T WAIT FOR A REACTION FROM HER.

I remember, as before when I had very little communication with the girls, when I was in the group of people and starting a conversation with some unfamiliar or even unknown girl, I behaved very unnatural. I spoke some nonsense, I kept talking about everything she wanted, even about those topics which were not interested in me, I laughed at her jokes, even when I did not understand their meaning, and in general, I absolutely did not show what I was worth, and who I was. As a result, after some time, most of them have forgotten me, and could not even remember who I am and what my name is. I was not even being put to the friend zone. I was generally not taken seriously.

Once I made the decision, and gradually began to change my approach to building relationships with women, I was unmoved and stood firm on one - I am, as I am, and every woman have to accept my personality. By this, I do not mean that it can, you justify your timidity, shyness and modesty in dealing with girls. No. These qualities I eradicated, because they were not part of me, the version of my person, which I sought. I mean that no matter what, a woman in front of me, and what the situation - it is bound to respect my interests and my hobbies. I stopped to talk on topics that are not interesting to me. If I want to talk about fishing, which I love - I'm talking to a girl about fishing, and I do not think whether she likes it or not. After all, I say what I like, and what is important to me. If I want to do something - I do, and I do not think how she will react to it. If I want to touch to her, if I really do sincerely want to - I immediately do it. Yes, she can push me away and to be against something, but it's important for me - to be completely natural. And ultimately, now I understand - it is very, very true. By such a behavior you show your male rod, that you are a male, you've got their own powerful reality, and no one on this planet can make you doubt yourself.

I want to give you a task that will help you to be more natural in dealing with girls: next time, in dealing with a girl, not very close to you (I mean, not a sister, or friend) tell her about your latest achievement in your hobby (in extreme cases, in your job), for example, that you finally finished your first rap single, or painted a picture, which you have long painted. But there is only one condition - you need to talk about it as you would have been telling it to your best friend. Do not adjust to her! Speak freely! Try it, her response should surprise you!

4. THE WORDS DON'T MATTER.

Most common question I hear when it comes to dating a girl is ..."what should I tell her?" About what to communicate? What is the best pick up line? I think you have discovered yourself in these matters. It's all about me for sure, because before, I thought what I say, depends on EVERYTHING! It seemed to me that by saying that something is not right - she will make about you a definite conclusion, and will cease to communicate with you. So I always thought for a long time about what I will say, what topics we will raise, I've been thinking, if I should tell any of my jokes! Therefore, I have almost never used such a powerful weapon as humor in dealing with girls. I thought that with the first unfortunate joke, she will think that I have completely no sense of humor, and immediately will reduce my chances to zero. But over time, with practice and experience, I realized that what you say is not as important as how you say it. Girls - being more emotional and men - logical. It is a scientific fact, but for some reason, we tend to forget this. Friend, using logic and words - you will never drag a Woman into your bed! Even if you say that you have a brand new Ferrari in your garage and you are dressed in the most expensive suit, but at the same time, you are being shy and closed, your words will make no desirable effect (we do not consider the gold-diggers)! In my experience, I will say that the most important thing is to let the girl understand that you are: 1) mentally adequate, in general; 2) being with you is comfortable and safe; 3) you are confident in your words and actions. Even if you talk about some rubbish, but you will keep eye contact, you will not forget to touch her, and you will give her the right context, she will be feeling quite comfortable with you and she will not stop communication with you!

For practicing, set yourself a goal to talk this week with 5 girls about some trash (you can choose a topic yourself) within 5 minutes. You can keep a couple of questions on this topic in advance to look confident, and do not get embarrassed. The main rule - look into her eyes, and speak loudly and legibly, with confidence in voice. I bet, after this exercise, you'll exactly understand everything I wrote above :)

5. DON'T BE AFRAID OF A NEW EXPERIENCE, PRACTICE YOUR SKILLS WITH ANY WOMAN, AND BE THE MAXIMALLY SOCIAL.

One of the very first tasks I've done to myself after taking the decision to change my life by learning to easily talk and seduce a woman is a task of generally enlarging my circle of women I communicate with. I clearly understood that I was not developing as a male while communicating with my limited number of female mates, and sister, as I could. I started to gradually talking with everyone: with a female cashier in McDonald's, cleaning woman in the shopping mall, unknown girls in public transport! I started with a simple wishing for a good day! Then, gradually I became more confident and could ask the girl at the cash desk how was going and, and later I started saying them compliments! For me it was not very difficult, because these women understood that I am a buyer, or a simple passer-by, I do not impose an acquaintance, and it was not difficult for them to smile and answer! In such small situations, I certainly kept eye contact, and tried to keep myself easily and confident (as if it were my old friend)! And that I noticed that this socialization began to help me in acquaintances! I noticed that it became easier to start a conversation, keep eye contact and, in general, it became more confident to hold unfamiliar people! I went further, gave myself an installation that every time I appeared in a public place where many people are, I tried to relax as much as possible! I came to the conclusion that only when I'm relaxed, I can start a conversation with almost any person! Yes, it is sometimes ridiculous, sometimes people did not want to communicate with me, but in a relaxed state it was easy for me, and I did it playing without straining.

    I began to communicate not only with girls who are attractive to me externally. At the first opportunity, I was starting a conversation with absolutely any girl! Thereby gaining experience from communicating with completely different girls - active, modest, daring. When you are refused by a girl who is not particularly interested in you - you accept this, and are not disappointed, right? But when you are refused by a girl that you like, you feel shitty. And this is normal! I found a way to absolutely calmly react to any objections of girls that I like - to put myself in different silly situations with plenty girls that I do not like! So I learned to do absolutely idiotic, ridiculous things in front of the girl of my dreams, while feeling absolutely confident! After all, before that, I took many different reactions from girls who did not interest me, and then, that experience that I got from those situations, I used in real "battle"! I hope, my friend, you have grasped my idea, and you understand that communication with different people, even with different males, on different topics makes you more relaxed, confident and interesting! This experience makes you an interesting guy. Girls will feel your lightness, ease and they will want to plunge into your social world, where everything is easy and funny! Therefore, go out, and communicate with everyone, do not be afraid of new experiences and emotions! It will only help you!

6. GET RID OF SOCIAL PRESSURE! DON'T BE AFRAID TO LOSE!

At the very beginning, when I decided to change myself, to become more confident and relaxed in communication with the girls, I could not, trivially, take the first step, and always looked for the most ideal opportunity to approach and get acquainted. I was eager to catch the moment when we were alone, or when she would be without her girlfriends. I was afraid to act in public places, because I thought that in case of failure, everyone around will witness my failure. Social pressure oppressed me, and I could not drive myself away from the thought that when you meet a girl, everyone is looking at us, and they are waiting for my failure. A friend, to be honest, I do not have one method or magic advice, which will immediately free you from fear of losing. The realization that to everyone, in fact, just to spit on you and your actions - came to me after hundreds of acquaintances with the girls. But I'll try to describe to you the psychology that I have now, and which, perhaps, will very much help you in dating girls. Imagine the situation that you are standing in line at the supermarket, and you really liked the girl standing two meters away from you. She is alone, but there are a lot of people around you, you are standing in line, everyone will hear what you will talk about.

Now, of course, I do not think about all this. I just inhale more air, turn off the brain with unnecessary thoughts, come up and say "hello, are you here alone?" (As an example). But when I just getting started, one of my friends, who was then obviously more skilled in the topic of seduction than I, with my next stamping on the spot and fear of social pressure, asked me sharply: "Dude, I see that you're scared, but what's the worst that can happen when you approach her? What are you afraid of?" I do not remember exactly what I answered him, but when I got home I thought about this question, and I realized that the worst thing that can happen is not at all frightening me, and I'm not scared! Imagine, though it's very unlikely, but still, what she will say to you: "Man, back off, you're not my type!". Sharply, yes. But is this what really scares you? Is it really what will hurt you?! Man, I would rather take it as a joke, laugh at it, and go with a good mood rather than get upset about it. What a fool she is when she talks in such a manner! That's nice that it all ended, I really do not need such a damned wretch. That's all! The story is over! You've done your job, you walked over and took a step. Not all the girls to whom you approach are worthy of you, man. You realized that you need another, and forget about this. And what will people think, you ask? Indeed, what will they think at that moment? Never mind! Men, I give you a guarantee, at heart, will respect your courage. Only complete losers will want your failure, but they should not be thought of! And women, in turn, are usually on your side! After all, they know this feeling when they miss off the next acquaintance, and then regret it, because the guy was very even nothing! And they internally want you to succeed! But what is worth noting is that out of the total number of people around you, in reality, there will be at most 10% of you to listen to!!! Friend, everyone has their own problems and thoughts in their heads. This will not be written in newspapers, and the result of your communication will not be shown on TV. Therefore, concentrate only on yourself, and on the fact that if you have a desire, you must act. You are a free man, you are in a free country, and if a man has a desire to get acquainted with a woman - this is absolutely normal, and any adequate person will take it as a fact. So do not worry, everything is much easier!

And...to achieve ease and comfort at dating the girls I had to eat more than one spoonful of shit, buddy. I made my experience gradually, step by step. And what I'm grateful for is that in my practice, I did not look at dating as white and black. I was not categorical that if dating ended in sex - it's a success, and if she did not even give her phone number - it's a total failure. Not at all! I appreciated, and rejoiced at every step and new experience! After so many negative reactions, I internally accepted this as part of the process! After all, when you learn something, let's say to drive a car, you do not get it all right, do you? You stall, you can confuse the pedals, but if you have a goal - in the end, it's easy and confidently to drive a car, you do not pay attention to it, but just try to go further! Absolutely everything is also in relation to the art of seduction, friend. To some extent, you must internally keep and accept the fact that she can refuse you. That she can have a man, she has a bad mood or something else. In general, you must accept something that you will not get to know each other. And the important thing is that only when you accept this, and keep in mind the fact that you can lose - you start to succeed! You absolve yourself of this responsibility, that you must definitely meet her, and fuck her. It becomes easier for you, you are relaxed, she sees that you are not attached to the result, and acquaintance for you is something ordinary, and you do not attach great importance to it. You can lose, I can lose, and so in everything in life, not only with women. And what, is it worth to be afraid of it? Of course not! It is worth to act, gain new experience and become more confident! And then the car will precisely fire up and will go quickly and confidently! ;)

7. FOCUS ON SUCCESSES, NOT FAILURES. ENJOY THE PROCESS, AND BE POSITIVE.

One of the principles that can just amplify the effect of your dating with women is a positive mindset. Anytime and anywhere. Under any circumstances. Now, unlike what was even 3 years ago, I do not see any failures as such. They simply do not exist. If I set myself the task to get acquainted during the day with 20 girls (although I have already not set myself such tasks for a long time), and 15 will just reject me, 4 just give a phone, and only one will go on a date with me and we'll get laid eventually - this great! I do not perceive 15 'failures' as failures. I perceive this as the fact that 15 crazy women have missed the opportunity to spend an excellent time with a cool guy! That's all! In each approach, I focus only on positive aspects, on those moments from which I had pleasant emotions and memories. Of course, if I fucked up, and I feel it, I draw conclusions, and I'm admitting honestly to myself about this error. But this is literally thoughts lasting 1-2 minutes! That's all! I do not remember this anymore! And the next day I will in every possible way block my brain and do not even remember those 15 refusals yesterday! Instead, with great pleasure, I will remember in myriad details my successful acquaintance, and how cool it was then! That's all! On my own experience, I can say that the focus only on one's actions and attempts - this leads to development! Looping on failure - does not move you further on any single step!

With this attitude, each your acquaintance must pass in the state of banter and the positivity radiated by you! Friend, when I meet in different situations with women right now, I do not set for myself the goal of fucking her or taking her phone by any means. My main task is to show myself, and have fun! Any objections and negatives will break against the wall of my positive attitude and self-confidence! If she says that I am the last goat on this planet, I will only smile at her, and I will say that there is a couple of ones who are worse, but I have every chance to get around them! If she says that I have an absurd hairstyle, I will laugh, and I will say that I have been making this hairstyle for 1.5 hours and consider her to be the fuckiest of my hairstyles! And in general, our common child with her, if it is a boy, will certainly come with such a hairdo!!! It is very important for me that we talked about what I like! As a rule, I set the tone and the mood of communication! In this spirit, even if we talk about her fucking boss, which I am not interested in at all, it will be full of fun! And in any case, I'll be in a good mood after that. Thus, friend, I lead you to the fact that you should not be able to get acquainted with unfamiliar women as something terrible and full of stress! Look at this as a small show and an adventure! Do not be afraid to seem stupid, just have fun. And I assure you, you will look at the general process of seduction quite differently, and each new acquaintance will be given much easier.

A couple of practical tips: hyperbolize criticism and any objections of girls. At the initial stage when you have little experience, you will be afraid of criticism and will be emotionally unstable towards any of her "No." If she says that she does not want to get acquainted with you, say "I'm not to get acquainted, I am telling you about myself, then we'll move to your person" or if she says that "you have a strange job", answer "I have the worst job out of all possible ones, but only it will bring me millions of dollars, there's nothing I can do about it." Yes, to some extent this may be a bit unnatural at first, but it will quickly instill emotional stability in you, you will not attach importance to her objections, and you will be able to keep your positive attitude under any circumstances.

8. ADVANCE TO THE END! PERSISTENCE IS THE KEY TO SUCCESS WITH WOMEN.

Of all the above-mentioned principles, this one, in my opinion, is the closest to the magic tablet you have cherished. Of course, this is also worth working on, it does not come in a day or two. But this is exactly what every male is able to do, and what really pleases women, fascinates them, and eventually, get laid in your bed. This is perseverance. Ability to keep your position, your desire and bring it to the mind of a woman in any way. This is the ability not to react to resistance, to refuse or resist you. Of course, when I had little experience, even at the earliest stage, when I parted with my beloved girlfriend, I was not persistent in getting to know women. I understood that this was important, but all my attempts were more like a need, and I looked more pitiful than insistent. And I want to share a key difference with you, my friends. To be persistent is to clearly understand what you want, to be able to bring it to the girl's consciousness, and let her know that it will happen, one way or another, but it will happen. This is the ability to listen to a girl and understand her position, but competently build your behavior and show her that your situation is more pleasant and profitable for her! This fascinates the girls, internally, most women do not want to decide anything, they want to be led, they want the guy to have everything under control. This realization in their head that you know the plan, and you always go on it, bypassing - any obstacles - they really like, because by that, she knows that with you she will be calm and confident. Unlike the state of need, when you show that you need something from the girl, and you are just stupidly begging her about it, I noticed that women are more inclined to men who are able to present those desires to the woman as one of the options of development of events, and as a rule, the most pleasant one for both of you! So do not ask the girl "Come to my house.", it is better to tell her "I'm planning to cook a duck with oranges today. I will buy wine, and I also have grapes brought from Greece, come and have supper with me. " Thus the girl herself will agree with desire by your development of events.

Of course, buddy, you can say that this is not easy. And I agree with you. To be persistent and adamant with every woman is very difficult, and requires a lot of practice. But since I mentioned the magic pill, I want to tell you what needs to be done, so that the same persistence will manifest itself in you more often! And this advice sounds like this: "Try to advance to the end." I mean, friend, try not to be limited to the lightest scenario. When I first started to get acquainted with women, I was usually limited to a half-minute conversation, I asked for her phone number, and immediately said goodbye and ran away! Even when I did not have any further business, I left these women! And this, friend, was a big mistake! It's silly to leave a woman, even when you took her contacts. The phone number itself is worthless, do not you agree? You want to call her then, or write and meet, go on a date? Or just drink something together? So why not to do it right away on acquaintance? If you communicate, you took her contacts, but she has free time, why not go and drink coffee with her? Thus, giving yourself more time to show yourself, to know her better, and to understand if she really likes you or not! Thus, you show her that you are not the next guy who takes the phone and does not call! You show your interest in her, the desire to spend time with her, which of course creates some comfort! The next time you are with her on a date, prepare everything in advance so that if possible, do not limit yourself to the initial script in the form of a date! After all, if she went with you on a date, you are interesting to her, and it is possible that you will have sex! Even on the same day! Therefore, prepare a place in advance, and at an opportunity, do not be afraid to act and invite her to go out with you! Friend, you do not even know how many girls I lost without doing it before! Did you meet at the club while sitting at a table? Down with just communication! Invite her to go and have a drink with you! And then go dance with her! You do not know the limits of her desires until you start acting and moving yourself! Very rarely when girls show their true intentions to the guys! They want sex as much as we do, that's for sure! But they will not show it! After all, they are afraid to look like sluts available. Therefore, buddy, this is our burden! Go to the end, but do not rush! Think what further is the appropriate continuation of your relationship, and can this be done now? Tomorrow? Look at her reaction, and try to go to the end!

Task: next time when you will get acquainted with the girl, do not just limit yourself by her phone number or contacts. Ask her what she is planning to do, and if she is not against drinking coffee with you! Now! If she thinks and breaks, say that you know a good place near (know in advance the concrete one)! Tell her that there is a great coffee, and invite her there! Over and over again doing this task, you will learn how to use the most from the situation, and more and more of your acquaintances will end up with sex! Take Action!

***

And now I want to briefly tell a story that happened to me several years ago, during a trip with my friends to Croatia. I have accumulated a lot of similar stories, but I want to share this one, since it contains practically all the principles that I have described above. Of course, such dating and results in the end, do not always happen, but in my opinion it will give you a better idea of the principles that help me in a pick-up practice, and maybe it will be good motivation for you!

So, I then have already practiced 2 or 3 years in the art of seduction, my friends were also in the "theme," so on Friday night we went to the biggest club in Zagreb, had a party, and had fun with the local beauties who were already very hot! I have never seen so many beautiful girls anywhere, as in Croatia. Brunettes, blondes, mouth-watering forms, attractive faces, and most importantly, just incredible openness to foreigners! In a sense, it's a man's paradise. We had a lot of day dates with couple of babes to go to the nearest bar near our hotel and seduce some of them. But my friends wanted to party in the club, and I wanted to see what it is like, the nightlife of Zagreb, so no one calling, we went to the club with our male company (4 guys).

There was a lot of people as always, in the countries of this part of Europe, the girls were dressed just super sexy, thereby attracting maximum attention. I will not tell everything in detail, I'll try to briefly go to the point, and focus on the key points. So, despite a large number of sexual chicks, the night did not come up and one by one, as if by conspiracy, they did not come into contact with me, and the night game somehow did not work out. Friends had almost the same result, someone was acquainted with someone, danced, drank a couple of cocktails, but when trying to translate the context into a more intimate channel, everything collapsed, and my friends were left alone. Laughing at some strange start of our club night, we ordered a bottle of whiskey, and sat down in the corner of the club, relax and drink (then I still drank alcohol). So we sat a little more than an hour, and again went to the dance floor. But to my greatest surprise, the situation was unchanged - I approached, got acquainted with the girl I liked, we started to dance, communicate, but as soon as I started more open communication and expressed my intentions (take a walk in the night city and come to my hotel, drink an excellent French wine), one after another immediately have merged. After wandering around the club for a while, and not stumbling upon something interesting, I returned to my friends for a table.

So a couple of hours passed, the party was nearing completion, people started to disperse and a couple of my friends expressed a desire to go to the hotel to sleep, because tomorrow morning we planned to get up early and go to the coast. After asking them to sit for a while, I walked away from the table so that I could see all those present at the club. "Man, make a last attempt, the night did not come up, but now you must be as persistent as possible, and act more resolutely. All the same, there is not much time, everyone leaves, and you too soon need to fall asleep. Therefore, there is nothing to hesitate" - I thought, and I stumbled upon a pretty brunette at the other end of the club. She shook her hips in time with the music, while her friends sat next to her and drank. "She's cool. She's hot! It is worth trying " - with such thoughts, I began to make my way to the brunette. Here I want to emphasize your attention, my friend, on my mind, namely, that internally I was not particularly affected by the negative results of this night, and despite the complete fall of the spirit of friends, I still wanted to get success that night. I was not hurt by refusals, I was sure that I simply did not act decisively, and with another attempt to me success will come *(principle 7)*.

- "Hello, your friends will booze and sit till evening, and your dancing enthusiasm will quickly disappear. I have the same situation, and I do not want to admit it. I'm Mateo" - I held out my hand to the brunette, in the hope that she understood my English.

- "Hello" - the brunette said coldly, hardly glancing at me and continuing to leave me.

Without thinking twice, I approached her from the other side and looking straight into her eyes said: "We go to the center of the dance floor. Here, in the corner of the hall, no one will see what kind of fuck you are! "- with a wink at her, I began to sway to the rhythm with her.

- "Listen, I'm resting here with my friends, I'm fine. "- she answered in good English, and again a step away from me.

- "Did you wear such a sexy dress, shoes and made this beautiful hairstyle to stand here sadly all night? Let's go to the dance floor, I can offer you something more interesting", I said confidently with a smile and taking her by the hand, gently dragged her towards the center of the dance floor.

- "Fuck off, moron!" - she blurted out and pushed me.

"Hmm, it's the same, but I do not need to give up so quickly," I thought, and said:

- "Okay, maybe I've expressed my intentions too harshly. Let's try again, this time I'll first ask how your name is.

- "Julia," the brunette said coldly.

- "I'm Mateo," I said, rocking slightly in her body.

- "Are you here alone?" - everything is just as cold, but not without attention.

- "No, I'm with the same company as you, drinking friends, they're going to leave, but I asked to give me 10 minutes, since I saw you, and just could not leave you here so bored."

- "You can leave, I'm fine. My friend has a promotion, so we will celebrate. I'll be with them." - Showing the blonde (already well drunk), said Julia.

- "Excellent," I said, and went towards the blonde *(principle 5!)*. She was sitting with a red-haired girl and a strong guy.

- Hi, I'm Mateo, and I found out that you were promoted. It is perfect! Congratulations! Blurted the blonde.

- "Thanks buddy!"

- "Your friend Julia says you do not want to let her dance."

- "Yes, we are celebrating."

- "You see, she's in a sad mood. She needs to dance with a great guy like me. In 10 minutes I will bring her to you."

- "Dude, we are together all night..."

- "10 minutes, and she's yours, in a good mood."

- "What do you want from me?"

- "Just nod" - with those words I went to Julia, who was interested in us.

- "Your friend said that I'm cool, and we should dance, let's go."

- "I do not want to dance with you," she said, but at that moment she looked at her friend, who pointed a finger at the dance floor.

"Whizz" - I thought, and taking Julia's hand, again dragged her to the dance floor. With some resistance, the brunette followed me. At first we danced rather detached from each other. I realized that I needed to show my adequacy, but do not go away and express direct intentions. We talked for a few minutes about me. Politely asking the same thing, I complimented her that she was the most beautiful in this club and held her on the waist (do not be afraid to lose!).

- "Thank you," Julia said, and began to rock her hips slightly towards me.

Feeling a crack in the ice, I started to move more actively. After dancing for about 5 minutes, letting her get used to me, I took her hand and dragged her on the stage, where there was a DJ, and dancing the bravest visitors of the club. In a few minutes, we danced together listening to the tracks of Armin van Buren. My hand was still on her waist, and as I approached, I pressed Julia more and more towards me. Leaning against me once more, I noticed her bright red lips, and, feeling a wild gust, immediately kissed her. Not expecting such a sharp step, the girl was trying to pull away from me, but feeling that I was holding her from behind, relaxed and continued the kiss. After that, we already touched each other in the dance for completely different places. Having stayed that scene for a while, in addition to the kiss, it is worth noting an important point. Being really very outwardly attractive, tanned, bright brunette, she attracted the attention of every man. But despite my presence, on the stage, twice, dudes approached her, and tried to take her away. To which I was strongly rebuffed and my cold: "She is with me" *(principle 1 and partially 8)*. After that, I caught up with her. But despite this, dancing a few more minutes, Julia began to ask her friends, "because they can worry where she disappeared." Descending from the stage, she, holding my hand, led to the table of her friends. Letting go of it, I approached my boys. They were going to leave, but they gave me another 5 minutes. Approaching Julia's table, I saw that her friends are slowly going to leave. Taking her by the hand, I immediately blurted out:

- "And you're going to leave me? I stayed with you for so long, all the local beauties have seen me with you, and now you're going to leave me?"

- "Mateo, I have to go, my friends are already leaving, one of my friends is bad", she said. "I have to go with them."

- "Three of them, your friends will take her home." And you stay, we will make this night magical *(what kind of nonsense I then said! Principle 4 in action!)* - by attaching it to the waist, I clung to her lips.

Stroking her on the back, I felt her hands on her chest, touching her, she asked:

- "Do you work out at the gym?"

Without thinking for a long time, I lightly took her hand and put it on my groin. Stopping the kiss, Julia smiled, and without removing her hands asked:

- "How do you rate this?"

- I think you'll like not only my breasts - firmly with a grin I squeezed her buttocks.

- "Are you so impudent?"

- "Half an hour ago you repelled me, but nevertheless, now you hold my dick. I do not care" *(principle 1, 8)*.

Smiling, Julia kissed me on the cheek:

- "I have to go ..."

At that moment I felt a push in the back, and as someone's hand took it and began to pull Julia to her. There was a key moment. The dude interfered with Julia's company and started to run into me, saying that they are leaving, and Julia is going with them. Not seconds without a bag, I closed it myself, and said that she would stay with me. The guy pushed me on the shoulder and said that they came together and will go away together, to which I told him that as she decides, so be it. I ignored his opinion. Turning, I looked inquiringly at the girl. I saw Julia's hesitation, as she looked at me and at him. At that moment I took her hand and whispered: "You know that you cannot leave now," feeling that the girlfriend is not bending over to his scales, the dude wanted to push me away from her, but then my friends approached him and said that he should let off steam. After calming down my boys, I looked at Julia, holding her hand. After pausing in 10 seconds, the girl told her friend that she would stay a little longer, that they could go and that they should not be worried about her. To which he reacted with another jerk at me, I calmly pushed him away and said coldly: "She made her choice, she stays here." Having tasted a little, the dude returned to his girlfriends, Julia approached them and said goodbye to them to the exit. Despite the fact that she went out into the street, I was obsessed with the certainty that she would return. After 5 minutes, she was not there. Sitting at her table, I firmly decided to wait for her. My friends said that she will not return, and they left. Saying goodbye to them, I said that I would wait for her, I was sure that she would return. After waiting another 5 minutes, when the cup of patience has already begun to stagger, she still came:

 - "Friends did not let go, could not escape..."

 - "I respect your choice. And I like him", I told her, and immediately kissed her.

Left alone, I completely freed myself, let my hands go. I saw that she liked it, she responded, touched me wherever she wanted. "It's amazing," I thought, "but it all started against me. I could just walk away from her. At first, she did not give me a chance." After spending 15 minutes with her at the club, we drank a cocktail and on my offer to drink excellent French wine in my hotel, she answered: "with pleasure," thereby making my night from a failed start, just enchanting. Julia was very passionate, and did not disappoint my expectations about the Croatian girls. They were incredibly hot. Soon, my friends confirmed it :)

After that, when I came to Zagreb, Julia called me to her house for dinner, we drank wine, and relaxed. And I still remembered this incident for a long time. In fact, earlier I would leave from its first refusal. I punched her wall with my perseverance. Showing her his interest, I let her know that, that night I was her best alternative. I did not give a chance to any man in that club, and she appreciated it. I said that I wanted to, and I was not afraid to lose (frequent touches, and the moment with the groin). I found a way to eliminate the problem in the form of a friend (I was not focusing on failures) and the night I took to myself. And most importantly, I got an incredible pleasure from the process, and even her friend's aggressive behavior could not provoke me to negativity and conflict. I did not want to lose what I wanted.

This story, friend, emphasizes the importance of the 8 principles I set out in this book. I came to each of them gradually, through the experience of failures and mistakes. I broke my comfort zone, only get close to understanding the truths that I systematized and shared with you in this book. In the complex, developed each of them, you will become an unequivocally more confident and free man. In the end, communication, dating and seduction of women will be for you a simple and natural experience. Therefore, friend, take these principles into service and use them right from today. You are a man, and worthy of having women that you like. Not everything will be easy. Nothing big does not happen only by positive emotions. But in due time I made a decision that changed me. The decision that helped me go through many difficulties, through my own fear and inability to communicate with women. And now, my experience through short key truths should help you to go this way easier and faster. And I'm sure you will succeed. Take Action!

Thank you for reading my book! I hope you learned a lot of valuable information for yourself!

By writing this book, I sincerely wanted to convey all the basic principles that I derived from my many years of experience in the pickup. But I understand that even after reading this book, you probably still have a few questions. Therefore, in order to bring you the maximum value, I'm leaving here my personal email, to which you can write any of your questions, and I will personally answer it.

info.mateolambert@gmail.com

In addition, I already have an idea for my next book, and in reply to your letter I will attach a small, but very valuable part of my next book in pdf format. I'm sure you'll like it!

Printed in Great Britain
by Amazon

27935710R00030